Using AI to Your Advantage

A Handbook for Putting AI Solutions into Practice for Growth and Efficiency

Taylor Royce

DEDICATION

To those who see a better future where technology advances humanity in hitherto unthinkable ways.

To the innovators who push the boundaries of imagination and the unsung heroes who work endless hours behind the scenes to achieve the seemingly unachievable.

I want to express my gratitude to my friends and family for their unwavering support and encouragement in all of my activities.

And to the readers, whose boundless curiosity and eagerness to learn foster progress and revelation. It is you who is making this effort.

CONTENTS

DISCLAIMER

This material is only meant to be used for informative and educational purposes. It is not meant to replace expert counsel or act as financial, legal, or medical advice. It is recommended that readers get guidance from qualified experts that are particular to their situation.

Although every attempt has been taken to guarantee the completeness and accuracy of the information provided, no implied warranties or guarantees are made. The use of or reliance on the information included in this publication may result in losses, injuries, or damages for which the author and publisher shall not be liable.

The opinions stated are the author's alone and may not represent those of any group or other body.

Before acting on any information, users are recommended to independently verify it. The content may be updated, changed, or removed by the author at any moment and without previous warning.

ACKNOWLEDGMENTS

I want to express my sincere gratitude to everyone who contributed to the creation of this work.

To my editor: I appreciate all of your effort, wise counsel, and tenacity in assisting me in refining my book to its highest standards. Without the expertise and dedication you have provided, this project would not have been feasible.

I am appreciative of my tech industry mentors and coworkers for sharing your knowledge and thoughts. Your opinions have broadened my understanding and greatly influenced the content of the book.

I want to express my gratitude to my family and friends for their unfailing support and patience while I was writing. Your strength and support have been a huge help.

Readers, thank you for your attention and questions. Your passion for technology motivates me to research new ideas and share them with the world.

In summary, this work pays homage to the unwavering quest of progress made by all the innovators and thinkers who continue to push the boundaries of what is conceivable. I appreciate how you've inspired me and a lot of other people to imagine and create a better future.

CHAPTER 1

Explaining Artificial Intelligence

1.1 What is AI, or artificial intelligence?

Artificial Intelligence, or AI for short, is the mimicking of human intelligence in robots through human-like programming of thought and learning. With the use of this technology, machines are now able to carry out operations like speech recognition, visual perception, language translation, and decision-making that would typically require human intelligence. The ultimate goal of artificial intelligence is to build self-sufficient systems that are capable of decision-making and performance improvement across time via data and experience learning.

The goal of artificial intelligence (AI) is to build machines that can replicate cognitive processes including language comprehension, learning, reasoning, and problem-solving. A variety of academic fields, including computer science, mathematics, psychology, neurology, and linguistics, are combined in the development of artificial intelligence. Large datasets, sophisticated algorithms, and potent computer systems have allowed artificial intelligence (AI) to progress from basic rule-based systems to sophisticated models that can recognize patterns and make complex decisions.

1.2 Various AI Types: Natural Language Processing, Deep Learning, and Machine Learning

The field of artificial intelligence is wide and includes many different subfields and approaches. Machine learning, deep learning, and natural language processing are three important areas of artificial intelligence that have attracted a lot of interest.

Intellectual Property (IP)

The creation of algorithms that allow computers to learn from and make predictions or judgments based on data is the emphasis of the machine learning subset of artificial intelligence. Machine learning algorithms find patterns and relationships in data to provide predictions that are well-informed, in contrast to traditional programming, which follows explicit instructions. Three primary categories of machine learning exist:

- Supervised Education: This method pairs the input data with the appropriate output, allowing the model to be trained on labeled data. By looking for patterns in the data, the algorithm learns how to translate inputs into outputs. Spam email filtering and picture recognition are two common applications.

- Unsupervised Education: In this instance, the model is trained on unlabeled data, which means that the algorithm must find patterns and connections in the data without being given clear instructions on what the desired result should be. Commonly utilized techniques in applications like market basket analysis and consumer segmentation are clustering and association.

- Reinforcement Learning: In this kind, an algorithm is trained by making mistakes and learning to make a series of judgments by getting feedback from its actions in the form of incentives or penalties. It is frequently utilized in autonomous driving, gaming, and robotics.

Deep Learning

Deep Learning is a niche branch of machine learning that uses many-layered neural networks—thus the name "deep" By using hierarchical feature extraction, these deep neural networks can learn intricate data representations. Deep learning has enabled major breakthroughs in tasks that require complex pattern detection and understanding, revolutionizing industries like computer vision, natural language processing, and speech recognition.

Intelligent Systems: Neural networks, the basis of deep learning, are modeled after the architecture and operations of the human brain. They are made up of layers of networked nodes, or neurons. In order to produce the intended output, each layer processes the incoming data, extracting features and sending them to the subsequent layer.

Language Processing (Natural): A branch of artificial intelligence called natural language processing studies how people and computers communicate using natural language. Enabling machines to comprehend, decipher, and produce meaningful and practical human language is the aim. NLP processes and analyzes vast volumes of natural language data by fusing machine learning and computational linguistics.

- Text Interpretation: The objective of these tasks, which include entity recognition, topic modeling, and sentiment analysis, is to extract meaningful information from text.

- Machine Translation: NLP makes it possible for text to be automatically translated between languages, promoting cross-lingual communication.

- Auditory Identification: With the help of this technology, spoken language can be translated into text for use in services like transcription and voice-activated assistants.

1.3 Advantages of Using AI Solutions

There are several advantages to using AI solutions in a variety of fields. Among the principal benefits are:

1. Productivity and Efficiency: Artificial intelligence (AI) systems have the speed and accuracy to process massive amounts of data, automating monotonous operations and freeing up human resources for more strategic endeavors. Businesses and industries benefit from higher production and efficiency as a result.

2. Improving Judgment-Taking: Massive data sets can be analyzed by AI to find trends and insights that people would overlook. This skill improves outcomes in industries including marketing, finance, and healthcare by enabling more informed and data-driven decision-making.

3. Reduction of Costs: AI can lower operating expenses by streamlining procedures and automating

operations. For instance, AI-powered predictive maintenance may detect equipment breakdowns and minimize downtime, saving industrial settings a substantial amount of money.

4. Introduction: AI enables the development of extremely customized user experiences. AI algorithms are used in e-commerce to evaluate user behavior and preferences and make product recommendations based on personal preferences. AI in healthcare can offer individualized treatment programs based on patient information.

5. New Prospects and Innovation: AI creates new avenues for innovation in many different sectors. It makes it possible to create hitherto unthinkable new goods, services, and business models. For example, in the pharmaceutical business, AI-driven research can expedite the development of new medications and therapies.

1.4 AI's Practical Uses in a Variety of Industries

Artificial Intelligence (AI) has impacted several industries, changing daily experiences and redefining company operations. Here are a few noteworthy real-world uses of AI in various industries:

1. Medicine: AI is revolutionizing healthcare in a big way, from bettering patient care to bettering diagnostics. Medical image analysis is used by machine learning algorithms to accurately identify diseases like cancer. Chatbots with AI capabilities help patients take control of their health by instantly responding to inquiries about medicine. AI systems also aid in the discovery of novel drugs by sifting through enormous datasets to find promising chemicals.

2. Money: AI is utilized in the financial industry for algorithmic trading, risk management, and fraud detection. Transaction data is analyzed by machine learning models to spot suspicious activity and stop fraud. AI-powered solutions enable more precise lending decisions by evaluating a borrower's financial history and behavior to determine

creditworthiness. AI is used by algorithmic trading systems to execute trades at the best times according to market conditions.

3. Sale: AI improves the shopping experience by managing inventory, making tailored recommendations, and providing customer support. AI algorithms are used by e-commerce platforms to make product recommendations based on user browsing history and preferences. AI-driven systems control inventory levels in physical stores, making sure shelves are filled with in-demand goods. Chatbots driven by AI offer immediate customer support by responding to questions and resolving problems.

4. Production: AI enhances production productivity and quality assurance. By using machine learning to forecast equipment failures and plan timely maintenance, predictive maintenance systems minimize downtime. Robots and automation systems driven by AI improve production lines by completing tasks quickly and precisely. Quality

control systems use computer vision to inspect items for flaws, ensuring high standards are maintained.

5. Movement: AI is revolutionizing transportation with its use in traffic management and driverless cars. Self-driving cars utilize AI algorithms to traverse roadways, avoid obstacles, and make real-time judgments, promising safer and more efficient transportation. AI-driven traffic management systems evaluate data from numerous sources to optimize traffic flow, minimize congestion, and improve overall transportation efficiency.

6. Education: AI is transforming education by enabling tailored learning experiences and automating administrative work. Intelligent teaching systems adapt to individual learning styles, giving individualized courses and feedback. AI-powered systems grade assignments and tests, lowering the workload for educators. Additionally, AI analyzes student data to detect learning gaps and offer treatments.

7. Entertainment: In the entertainment sector, AI enhances content production and recommendation systems. Streaming companies utilize AI algorithms to offer movies, TV episodes, and music based on user likes. AI-generated content, such as music and artwork, highlights the creative potential of machine learning. Additionally, AI-driven tools assist in editing and post-production processes, enhancing efficiency and quality.

Through a comprehensive understanding of artificial intelligence (AI), ranging from its foundational principles to its real-world applications, we can gain a deeper appreciation for the technology's transformative capabilities. Artificial Intelligence is more than just a sci-fi idea; it's a powerful technology that has already started to profoundly alter our environment.

CHAPTER 2

Determining Your Company's AI Requirements

2.1 Assessing Business Possibilities and Challenges

Doing a thorough assessment of your company potential and problems is an essential first step when integrating AI into your organization. This entails taking a close look at the areas in which your company is struggling, inefficient, or experiencing bottlenecks, as well as the areas where innovation, development, and progress are possible.

1. Identifying Pain Points: To determine the most urgent problems, start by getting feedback from different departments and stakeholders. These problems could include lengthy manual procedures, a high mistake rate, unsatisfied customers, or ineffective logistics. For example, AI-driven chatbots could be a great tool to help your customer care team if they are overworked and receiving a lot

of the same questions.

2. Investigating Prospects for Growth: AI is not just for solving problems; it can also open up new possibilities. Seek out opportunities to innovate or obtain a competitive advantage with AI. This might be forecasting market trends, improving product suggestions, or tailoring marketing campaigns. AI may evaluate customer data to find high-potential leads, for instance, if your sales force has trouble identifying the proper clients to target.

3. Interacting with Stakeholders: Key stakeholders from throughout the company must be engaged in order for assessment to be effective. To get ideas, do workshops, interviews, and brainstorming sessions with executives, managers, and staff. Their viewpoints will assist you in identifying the areas where AI can have the biggest influence. Make sure you comprehend the anticipated results as well as the current challenges.

2.2 Charting Processes to Integrate AI

After recognizing the obstacles and prospects, the following stage is to map your processes to ascertain the areas where AI can be successfully included. This entails examining your present workflows to pinpoint particular actions or stages that artificial intelligence (AI) can improve or automate.

1. Evaluating Existing Workflows: Start by thoroughly recording your current workflows. This entails outlining every stage of your workflow from beginning to end. If you are examining your supply chain management, for instance, make sure to record each step, from order fulfillment to inventory management. This will assist you in identifying areas of inefficiency or delays.

2. Identifying AI Integration Points: Next, locate locations where AI can be integrated into these operations. Look for jobs that can be automated that are time-consuming, repetitious, or prone to mistakes. Predictive maintenance enabled by AI, for

instance, can be used to reduce downtime in production settings by tracking the condition of equipment and anticipating breakdowns.

3. Developing a Comprehensive Plan for AI Implementation: Create a thorough plan for integrating AI. A detailed roadmap explaining how AI will be included into each workflow should be part of this. Think about the resources needed for implementation, the tools and technologies required, and the data needed to train AI models. If you're incorporating AI into your customer support procedure, for example, describe how the technology will handle client interactions and forward complex requests to human agents.

2.3 Setting Use Case Priorities for Implementing AI

Setting a priority list for these use cases is the next step after determining where AI can be integrated. Since not all AI initiatives are made equal, it's critical to concentrate on those that complement your strategic objectives and have the greatest potential return on investment (ROI).

1. Evaluating Effect and Viability: Consider the impact and viability of each possible AI use case when evaluating it. Impact describes the possible advantages, including cost reductions, increased productivity, or revenue development. The technical and operational obstacles, such as data accessibility, integration complexity, and necessary knowledge, are taken into account during the feasibility phase. A smaller project with immediate wins might be more viable than an AI project that promises large cost reductions but requires considerable data cleaning and integration.

2. According to Strategic Objectives: Make sure the use cases that are prioritized match the strategic objectives of your company. For instance, if your organization wants to increase customer happiness, give top priority to AI initiatives that help achieve this goal directly, like faster service response times or more individualized customer experiences. By coordinating AI projects with strategic objectives, you can make sure that your attention is on the

things that are most important to your company.

3. Building a Prioritization Matrix: Create a matrix of priorities to order your AI use cases according to their significance and viability. Stakeholders can better understand which initiatives to embark on first with the aid of this graphic tool. Projects with high impact and feasibility scores, for example, ought to be given priority; those with lower scores, on the other hand, should be postponed or need more planning.

2.4 Calculating the Benefits and Drawbacks

It is imperative to perform a comprehensive cost-benefit analysis prior to implementing AI. To guarantee a satisfactory return on investment, this approach entails weighing the possible expenses of AI initiatives against the anticipated benefits.

1. Estimating Costs: Compile a list of all expenses related to the use of AI. This covers both direct expenses like hardware and software as well as

indirect expenses like data preparation, training, and continuing maintenance. Consider the expenses associated with gathering the required data, creating the algorithm, and integrating it with your current systems, for instance, if you're implementing an AI-powered recommendation system.

2. Quantifying Benefits: Next, figure out how much the AI project is projected to benefit from. Benefits might be intangible (like better decision-making or higher customer satisfaction) or concrete (like higher revenue or lower operating costs). For example, a predictive maintenance system powered by AI might decrease equipment downtime, resulting in substantial cost savings and higher production.

3. Determining ROI: Compare the projected expenses and benefits to determine the return on investment. This entails dividing the outcome by the whole costs after deducting the total costs from the total benefits. For instance, the return on investment (ROI) would be 200% if an AI project were to be implemented for $100,000 and yield $300,000 in benefits.

4. Making Informed Decisions: Consider which AI initiatives to pursue based on the findings of the cost-benefit analysis. Prioritizing should go to projects that have a good fit with strategic goals and a positive return on investment. But take into account the possible risks and uncertainties, and be ready to modify your plans as necessary.

5. Iterative Evaluation: A cost-benefit analysis ought to be carried out on a regular basis. Continue to assess the costs and advantages of AI projects as they advance to make sure they stay feasible. By using an iterative strategy, you can optimize the return on your AI investments and adjust to changing conditions.

You may strategically apply AI to address issues, seize opportunities, and yield major benefits by using these methods to ascertain your organization's AI needs. Mapping workflows, identifying use cases, understanding your business needs, and conducting thorough cost-benefit analyses are all necessary to ensure that your AI initiatives are well-thought-out, aligned with your goals, and well-positioned for success.

CHAPTER 3

Putting Together an AI Group

3.1 Internal Knowledge: Engineers, Business Analysts, and Data Scientists

Finding and developing the appropriate internal knowledge is the first step in creating a successful AI team. Every position on the AI team contributes special abilities and viewpoints that are necessary for the effective application of AI.

1. Information Scientists: Any AI team's core is its data scientist. Their area of expertise lies in utilizing sophisticated machine learning algorithms and statistical analysis to obtain significant insights from huge datasets. Among their duties are:

2. Collection and Preparation of Data: Compiling and sanitizing data from diverse sources to guarantee its readiness for examination.

3. Model Building: Creating algorithms and predictive models with the ability to recognize patterns and make judgments or predictions based on data.

4. Evaluation: Examining how well models function in order to make sure they adhere to the required dependability and accuracy requirements.

To draw and keep the best data science talent, provide competitive pay, chances for further education, and an exciting work environment. Through workshops, conferences, and online courses, encourage data scientists to stay up to date with the newest tools and approaches in AI and machine learning.

1. Engineers: AI engineers are essential to the implementation and upkeep of AI systems, especially those that specialize in software development and machine learning. Among their main responsibilities are:

2. System Integration: Including AI models into current business procedures and systems to make sure they work well with the infrastructure already in place.

3. Scalability: Creating scalable systems that maintain

performance even in the face of growing data and user volumes.

4. Maintenance: Consistently upgrading and caring for AI systems to guarantee their long-term efficacy and security.

Strong programming abilities in Python, R, and Java are essential for AI engineers, as is expertise with PyTorch and TensorFlow, two popular AI frameworks. By giving them access to the newest tools and technology and creating an atmosphere that welcomes experimentation and creativity, you can support their professional development.

1. Business analysts: Business analysts serve as a liaison between technical teams and stakeholders in the business world. They guarantee that AI projects produce measurable business benefits and are in line with company objectives. Among their duties are:

2. Requirement Gathering: Assisting stakeholders in determining business requirements and converting them into technical specifications for the AI team.

3. Performance Metrics: establishing key performance indicators (KPIs) to gauge AI project progress and

guaranteeing business goals are met.

4. Communication: Informing technical and non-technical stakeholders on a regular basis of project developments, difficulties, and accomplishments.

Business operations and AI capabilities should be well-understood by business analysts. Give them training so they can become more proficient in their technical areas and stay up to date with the most recent developments in the field.

3.2 Collaborating with Outside AI Consultants and Experts

Partnering with outside AI specialists and consultants can help develop internal expertise while also offering important insights, extra resources, and specialized knowledge that might not be available internally.

1. Selecting the Correct Partners: Select outside partners who have a track record of successfully using AI in your sector. Seek professionals who can

provide:

2. Strategic Advice: Advice on AI strategy that will assist you in setting priorities and allocating resources wisely.

3. Technical Expertise: Specific knowledge and talents that enhance the capabilities of your internal team, such as deep learning, computer vision, or natural language processing.

4. Implementation Support: Help with system integration, modification, and user training while implementing AI solutions.

Teamwork Projects

Involve outside parties in cooperative projects that promote skill and knowledge development. To obtain practical experience and acquire competence, include your internal team in the design and development phase of an AI-driven customer support chatbot, for example.

- Outsourcing and Contracting: When working on short-term or highly specialized projects, think about hiring outside experts to do particular duties. This strategy can reduce workload and introduce new ideas without requiring the long-term commitment of hiring more full-time employees.

3.3 Promoting a Collaborative and Innovative Culture

Establishing an environment that fosters creativity and teamwork is crucial to the success of your artificial intelligence projects. In order to do this, it is necessary to encourage open communication, cross-functional teamwork, and an experimental and failure-driven mindset.

1. Encouraging Teams with Different Functions: Create cross-functional teams with members that represent a range of departmental skill sets. To create a customized marketing campaign, an AI project team can consist of data scientists, engineers, business analysts, and marketing experts. By working together, we can make sure that AI solutions are comprehensive and meet the needs of different stakeholders.

2. Encouraging Honest Conversation: Create open

channels of communication so that team members can freely express their thoughts, opinions, and worries. This can be facilitated by holding regular meetings, brainstorming sessions, and using collaboration tools like Microsoft Teams or Slack. Promote an environment where inquiry and questions are encouraged and errors are seen as teaching opportunities.

3. Encouraging Innovation and Experimentation: Innovative environments that encourage experimentation and are forgiving of failure are conducive to innovation. Establish a sandbox setting so that groups can experiment with new concepts without worrying about making a quick profit. Honor creative problem-solving and original thinking in teams, even when the results aren't always favorable.

3.4 Continuous Education and Training Initiatives

Since AI is a sector that is always developing, keeping your team's skill set current is essential to having a competitive edge. Making continuous training and development investments guarantees that your staff is up to date on the newest developments and industry best practices in artificial intelligence.

1. Ongoing Educational Opportunities: Make a range of educational tools accessible, such as webinars, workshops, and conferences in addition to online courses. Specialized AI courses are available on platforms like Coursera, Udacity, and edX, which can assist your team in staying up to date with the newest techniques and technology. To increase their credibility and level of competence, team members should be encouraged to obtain certifications in pertinent fields.

2. Internal Training Programs: Create internal training initiatives that are tailored to your company's unique requirements. Interactive workshops, hackathons, and knowledge-sharing sessions where team members share what they've learned from previous conferences or projects are a few examples of these programs. Internal training contributes to the

development of a coherent grasp of AI applications that are pertinent to your company.

3. Coaching and Mentoring: Create programs for coaching and mentoring where team members with more expertise mentor and assist colleagues with less experience. This promotes a cooperative and encouraging work environment in addition to quickening the learning curve. Mentors are able to share best practices, offer insightful advice, and guide mentees through challenging AI problems.

4. Remaining Up to Date on Industry Trends: Encourage the members of your team to be up to date on the most recent developments in technology, research, and industry trends. Engage in AI communities and forums and subscribe to journals, blogs, and newsletters. Talk about new developments and how they might affect your company's AI strategy on a regular basis.

Your company may effectively manage the challenges of implementing AI by creating a well-rounded AI team with the appropriate balance of external partnerships and internal knowledge, encouraging a collaborative and innovative culture, and allocating resources for continuous skill development and training. By using this strategy, you can be confident that your team has the abilities, mindset, and understanding required to fully utilize AI and provide significant business results.

CHAPTER 4

Data: AI's Engine

4.1 Techniques for Gathering Data from Internal and External Sources

Artificial intelligence (AI) systems rely on data to learn, forecast, and make decisions. Strong data gathering techniques that use both internal and external sources are crucial for the success of your AI projects.

- Internal Data Sources: Information gathered via regular business activities can comprise a variety of data kinds that are contained within your organization. Internal data sources include, for example:

- Operational Data: This comprises details gleaned from your company's operational procedures, including supply chain management, customer service exchanges, and sales transactions.

- Customer Data: Information obtained from contacts with customers, including website visits, past purchases, and feedback forms.
- Employee Data: Details about internal conversations, HR documentation, and employee performance.

Make sure you have procedures in place for reliable and consistent data collecting if you want to optimize the value of internal data. This procedure can be streamlined by putting in place ERP (Enterprise Resource Planning) software, CRM (Customer Relationship Management) systems, and other data management tools.

1. External Data Sources: Information gathered from sources outside your company can offer insightful context and extra information. Some instances of outside data sources are:
2. Public Databases: Industry reports, government databases, and research studies can provide a plethora of pertinent industry-related information.
3. Social Media: Websites like LinkedIn, Facebook, and Twitter are excellent resources for information

on consumer attitudes and industry trends.

4. Third-Party Data Providers: Organizations that focus on gathering and analyzing data can offer comprehensive datasets customized to meet your requirements.

You can have a deeper insight of your market, rivals, and consumer behavior by utilizing external data. Additionally, it can close any gaps in your internal data, giving your AI models a more complete picture to work with.

4.2 Cleaning and Preparing Data for Quality Control

To guarantee data quality and applicability for AI applications, it is imperative to clean and preprocess data after it has been acquired. It is crucial to take the time to complete these procedures since low-quality data can result in erroneous models and insights.

- Data Cleaning: Cleaning up your dataset entails finding and fixing mistakes, inconsistencies, and inaccuracies. Typical duties in data cleaning consist of:

- Removing Duplicates: Making sure that duplicate records are found and eliminated in order to avoid results that are biased.

- Handling Missing Values: Managing data gaps by eliminating incomplete records or imputed values that are appropriate.

- Correcting Errors: Finding and fixing typos and improper formatting in data entry errors.

For instance, if you have client data that is lacking email addresses, you may decide to either remove the incomplete entries if they are not essential or use information from other records to fill in the gaps.

- Data Preprocessing: Preprocessing data converts unprocessed data into a format that artificial intelligence algorithms can understand. This action consists of:

- Normalization and Standardization: Data scaling to guarantee uniformity, particularly in the case of numerical values with varying units or ranges.

- Encoding Categorical Variables: Putting numerical representations of categorical data (such as product categories or gender) into a manner that AI systems can understand.

- Feature Engineering: Adding new features or changing current ones to improve your model's capacity for prediction.

For example, you may extract variables such as the day of the week or month from a dataset that contains transaction dates in order to find trends pertaining to client behavior.

Your AI models will be trained on dependable, high-quality data if you carefully clean and preprocess your data, which will produce more accurate and useful insights.

4.3 Handling Privacy and Data Security Issues

In managing data security and privacy, it becomes increasingly important as you gather, store, and process large volumes of data. Maintaining trust and shielding your company from potential breaches requires protecting sensitive data and making sure standards are followed.

- Data Security: Data security is safeguarding

information against hacker attacks, illegal access, and other online dangers. Important tactics consist of:

- Encryption: Encrypting data to guarantee its security even in the event of interception, both during transmission and at rest.

- Access Controls: Strict access controls should be put in place to guarantee that only individuals with permission can access sensitive information. Role-based access controls (RBAC) and multi-factor authentication (MFA) are two examples of this.

- frequent Audits: To find and fix any possible vulnerabilities in your data infrastructure, conduct frequent security audits and vulnerability assessments.

Encrypting customer data in your CRM system, for instance, guarantees that the information is unreadable by unauthorized parties even in the event of a breach.

- Data Privacy: Data privacy pertains to safeguarding the private information of persons and guaranteeing adherence to data protection laws like GDPR,

CCPA, and HIPAA. Important procedures consist of:

- Data Anonymization: Encrypting or removing personally identifying information (PII) to preserve personal privacy without compromising the ability to analyze data.

- Consent Management: Making sure you have people's express consent before collecting and using their data, as well as giving them the opportunity to opt out.

- Compliance Monitoring: Consistently examining and upgrading your data processes to guarantee adherence to pertinent laws and policies.

Anonymizing names and contact information, for example, can assist preserve customers' privacy while utilizing their data to train an AI model while still providing you with useful insights.

4.4 Constructing a Sturdy Data Architecture

Having a strong data infrastructure is essential for using AI effectively. It includes all of the processes, systems, and equipment needed to efficiently gather, store, process, and analyze data.

- Storage Options for Data: For huge data volumes to be managed securely and effectively, selecting the appropriate data storage solutions is essential. Choices consist of:

- On-Premises Storage: Actual servers housed in your company that provide you control over security but need a lot of upkeep.

- Cloud Storage: Cloud service providers like AWS, Google Cloud, or Azure offer scalable and adaptable storage options. These solutions provide strong security features and lower maintenance costs.

- Hybrid Solutions: Balancing control and scalability by combining cloud and on-premises storage.

For instance, cost and performance can be maximized by keeping frequently used data on-site for easy access while utilizing cloud storage for backup and archiving.

1. Data Processing Frameworks: Large dataset handling and analysis require the use of effective data processing frameworks. Important technologies consist of:

2. Hadoop: An open-source framework enabling huge data processing and storage across computer clusters in a distributed manner.

3. Spark: An efficient in-memory data processing engine that is useful for real-time analytics and large-scale data processing.

4. Data Pipelines: Automated processes that transfer data into your processing and storage systems from a variety of sources, making sure it is cleansed, converted, and prepared for analysis.

For example, real-time processing of streaming data from Internet of Things devices using Spark can yield instant insights and set off automated reactions.

1. Data Governance: Making sure your data is accurate, consistent, and used appropriately requires the establishment of effective data governance procedures. Important elements consist of:

2. Data Quality Management: Consistently assessing and refining data quality in order to preserve its dependability and utility.

3. Metadata Management: Providing context and

enhancing data discoverability through the documentation of data sources, structures, and usage.

4. Policies and Procedures: Establishing and implementing guidelines for the use, sharing, and access to data in order to guarantee adherence to laws and industry best practices.

One way to keep your datasets relevant and intact is to establish a data governance system that includes regular data quality assessments and explicit documentation of data sources.

You may lay a solid foundation for successful AI endeavors by comprehending the significance of data in AI, implementing efficient data gathering techniques, guaranteeing data quality through cleaning and preprocessing, attending to security and privacy issues, and constructing a strong data infrastructure. Your company will be able to drive innovation, effectively harness data, and produce significant business benefits with this all-encompassing approach.

CHAPTER 5

Selecting Appropriate AI Tools and Platforms

5.1 Comparing Proprietary and Open-Source AI Solutions

One of the first choices you'll have to make when starting an AI project is whether to use proprietary versus open-source AI solutions. Each has advantages and disadvantages that you should be aware of in order to make an informed choice that fits the needs and resources of your company.

Intelligent Software

Communities of developers create open-source AI technologies, which are freely used, modified, and distributed. TensorFlow, PyTorch, and Scikit-Learn are a few examples. Here are some advantages and things to think about:

- Economically Sound: The fact that open-source solutions are typically free to use can be a big benefit for businesses on a tight budget. On the other hand, implementation, modification, and upkeep could come with unstated costs.

- Adaptability and Personalization: These tools offer a great degree of customisation because they can be adapted to unique requirements. This is especially helpful if your project calls for certain features or capabilities that aren't found in proprietary software.

- Partnership Support: Strong community support is often included with open-source solutions. In addition to participating in forums, tutorials, and documentation, users can also influence the software's continuous development. In contrast to for-profit support services, there could be less accountability and a range in the quality of care.

- Safety and Dependability: Open-source solutions can be examined by a large audience because the code is publicly available, which could result in more dependable and safe software. Conversely, being open implies that weaknesses may be taken advantage of if they are not quickly fixed.

In-house AI Solutions

Commercial companies create and market proprietary AI solutions. Amazon SageMaker, Microsoft Azure AI, and IBM Watson are a few examples. These instruments have a unique set of benefits and things to keep in mind.

- All-Inclusive Support: Professional support services are frequently included in proprietary solutions, and they can be very helpful in troubleshooting and performance optimization. This can be especially helpful for companies without internal technological skills.
- Interfaces That Are Easy to Use: Usually created with the user experience in mind, these tools provide user-friendly interfaces and efficient workflows that help speed up deployment and lower the learning curve.
- Compatible Features: The integrated tools and services that are frequently included with proprietary solutions help streamline the entire AI development

and implementation process. But this might result in vendor lock-in, which makes it difficult to interface with other tools or move providers.

- Price: Cost is the primary downside. With license fees, subscription prices, and extra charges for upgrades and maintenance, proprietary systems can be costly.

5.2 Cloud-Based AI Services and Platforms

The way businesses create and implement AI solutions has been completely transformed by cloud-based AI platforms and services. These platforms offer a variety of cloud-hosted tools and services, with the following benefits:

1. Accessibility and Convenience: Teams can work together effortlessly no matter where they are thanks to cloud-based AI platforms, which are accessible from any location with an internet connection. Teams that operate remotely or companies that have rules allowing remote work would especially benefit from this.

2. Achievability of scaling: Scalability is one of cloud-based AI technologies' most important benefits. By swiftly adjusting their resources in response to demand, organizations may make sure they are only paying for what they utilize. Projects with varying workloads or seasonal fluctuations benefit greatly from this flexibility.

3. Economy of Cost: Organizations can avoid the upfront expenditures of buying and maintaining hardware by utilizing the cloud. Pay-as-you-go models are available from cloud providers and can be more economical, particularly for smaller businesses or those with erratic usage patterns.

4. Ecosystem and Integration: Cloud service providers such as AWS, Google Cloud, and Microsoft Azure provide whole ecosystems that encompass data storage, analytics, and other services in addition to AI technologies. Workflows may be streamlined, and AI projects can operate more efficiently overall, thanks to this integration.

Cloud-Based AI Platform Examples:

- Amazon SageMaker: A fully managed service that handles every step of the machine learning process, from preparing data to deploying models.
- Google Cloud AI Platform: Offers access to Google's cutting-edge AI technologies as well as tools for creating, implementing, and maintaining machine learning models.
- Microsoft Azure AI: Provides a selection of AI tools and services, such as bot services, machine learning, and cognitive services, that are connected with the larger Azure ecosystem.

5.3 Taking AI Tools' Scalability and Flexibility into Account

It's critical to take into account an AI tool's scalability and flexibility when selecting it to make sure it can grow with your organization's demands and adapt to various projects and requirements.

Scalability

- Vertical scaling: relates to boosting the capacity of current resources (e.g., upgrading servers). This can help with demanding AI activities that demand a lot of processing power.

- Horizontal Scaling: Consists of increasing resources (e.g., servers) in order to manage increasing workload. This method can increase redundancy and fault tolerance and is frequently more economical.

Be sure the AI technologies you use are capable of managing both kinds of scaling. Excellent scalability is a feature of cloud-based platforms in general, enabling you to scale resources up or down as needed without incurring large delays or costs.

Adaptability:

- Multipurpose Applications: Seek for artificial intelligence (AI) solutions that can be used for a variety of tasks, such as recommendation systems, computer vision, natural language processing, and predictive analytics. Due to its adaptability, you won't need to buy numerous specialist tools, which might save you money and time.

- Interoperability: Integration with other tools and systems is an essential skill. Selecting AI technologies that facilitate smooth integration with your current technological stack requires support for common standards and APIs.

- Adjustment: The capacity to modify instruments to meet your unique requirements is another aspect of flexibility. While proprietary solutions may offer more out-of-the-box capabilities but less flexibility, open-source tools typically give greater customization choices.

5.4 Correlating Tools with Particular Use Cases and Data Needs

It's important to match your chosen AI technologies to your unique use cases and data needs when choosing them. This guarantees that the instruments you select can produce the required results and are appropriate for the job at hand.

Comprehend Use Cases

- Establish Goals: Clearly state the goals for your artificial intelligence project. Do you want to boost predictive maintenance, streamline supply chains, or provide better customer service? AI skills may vary depending on the goal.

- Determine Needs: Ascertain the particular needs of your use case. For instance, tools for text data handling and language models are needed for natural language processing projects, whereas tools for picture processing and analysis are needed for computer vision projects.

Assessing Data Needs

- Data Amount: Determine the amount of data you will be handling. Tools that have strong data handling and processing capabilities may be required for large datasets.

- Diversity of Data: Think about the many kinds of data you will work with: unstructured (text, photos) or structured (data, databases, etc.). Make sure the instruments you select are capable of handling and analyzing the particular data kinds.

- Quality of Data: Reliable data is essential for precise AI models. To make sure your data is ready for analysis, pick tools with features for quality control, preprocessing, and data cleansing.

Examples of Matching platforms to Use Cases

- Chatbot for Customer Service: Pre-built capabilities for conversational AI and natural language comprehension can be found in platforms like Microsoft Bot Framework and Google Dialogflow.
- Predictive Maintenance: Programs like IBM Watson IoT or Azure IoT Central can evaluate sensor data and forecast equipment breakdowns if your aim is to apply predictive maintenance in manufacturing.
- Analytics for Marketing: Tools that combine AI-driven analytics with customer relationship management (CRM) platforms, such as Salesforce Einstein or Adobe Sensei, are good choices for customized marketing efforts.

You can choose the best AI tools and platforms to support

your company's AI initiatives by carefully weighing the advantages of cloud-based platforms, open-source and proprietary solutions, scalability and flexibility, and matching tools to particular use cases and data requirements. With the best resources available, your AI projects will be more successful and have a greater impact thanks to this careful approach.

CHAPTER 6

Building and honing your AI model

6.1 Choosing the Right Type of AI Model (e.g., Regression, Classification)

One of the most important first steps in creating a successful AI application is choosing the appropriate kind of AI model. The decision is based on the kind of data you have and the nature of the problem you are attempting to address.

1. Classification Models: When the objective is to classify data into predetermined labels or classes, classification models are applied. When the solution is a discrete label, they are perfect. As an illustration:

- The process of classifying emails as either spam' or 'not spam.'

- Medical Diagnosis: Deciding whether or not a patient is afflicted with a disease.

- Customer Segmentation: Putting clients in groups according to their purchase patterns.

2. Regression Models: Unlike discrete categories, continuous values are predicted using regression models. When the output is a real number, they are employed. As an illustration:

- House Price Prediction: Calculating a home's estimated cost by taking into account factors including location, size, and amenities.

- Sales Forecasting: Projecting future sales using past performance information.

- Temperature Prediction: Making a weekly temperature prediction.

3. Clustering Models: Without predetermined labels, clustering models combine comparable data points. They are helpful in identifying groups and trends within data. As an illustration:

- client Segmentation: Making use of behavior to identify specific client segments for focused marketing.

- Document clustering involves assembling related

documents to facilitate information retrieval.

4. Recommendation Systems: These models forecast user preferences and provide suggestions in line with those predictions. Typical instances consist of:

- Product Suggestions: Making product recommendations based on previous purchases and browsing activity.
- Recommendations for Content: Making suggestions for articles, films, or music depending on user tastes.

5. Models of Natural Language Processing (NLP): NLP models deal with tasks associated with producing and comprehending human language. They are employed in:

- Sentiment Analysis: Identifying the sentiment—positive, negative, or neutral—that underlies a text.
- Machine Translation: Converting textual content between languages.
- Chatbots: Constructing conversational agents capable of comprehending and reacting to input from users.

The development process begins with selecting the right kind of model. To make the greatest decision, it's critical to specify the problem precisely and comprehend the kind of facts you're dealing with.

6.2 Model Training Process.

To guarantee that an AI model learns from data and produces correct predictions, there are multiple phases involved in training it. Data splitting, model training, performance validation, and accuracy testing are all steps in the process.

1. Dividing Data: Splitting your dataset into three primary sections is known as data splitting.

- Material for Training: Usually, the model is trained using 70–80% of the data. This is how the correlations and patterns in the data are taught to the model.

- Set of Validations: To adjust the model's parameters and determine the optimal model configuration, 10–15% of the data are employed. By doing this, overfitting is less likely to occur, where the model performs well on training data but badly on fresh data.

- Set for Testing: The performance of the model is assessed using the remaining 10–15% of the data. This data is not utilized in the training phase, guaranteeing an objective evaluation of the model's correctness.

2. Training the Model: In order to reduce error, the model's parameters are adjusted based on the training data. This includes:

- Feeding Data: Supplying the model with the training data.

- Learning Patterns: Modifying weights and biases through methods such as gradient descent.

- Iterative Process: To improve the model, repeat the procedure over a number of times (epochs).

3. Validation: By assessing the model's performance on the validation set, validation aids in fine-tuning it. Methods consist of:

- Hyperparameter tuning: Changing variables such as

batch size, number of layers, and learning rate to determine the ideal mix.

- Cross-Validation: To guarantee robustness and lower variance, the data is divided into several folds and multiple models are trained.

4. Examination: Testing the model on the testing set to assess its performance is the last stage. Among the metrics used to evaluate the model are:

- Accuracy: The proportion of accurate forecasts.
- Accuracy and Memory: Recall evaluates the capacity to locate all pertinent instances, whereas precision reflects the accuracy of positive predictions.
- F1 Score: An equilibrium between recall and precision.
- Mean Squared Error (MSE) and Mean Absolute Error (MAE): Regression model metrics used to calculate prediction errors.

6.3 Tracking Model Outcomes and Resolving Bias

To make sure your AI system keeps producing fair and

accurate outcomes, you must continuously monitor model performance. It entails monitoring important indicators and correcting any biases that might appear.

Performance Monitoring

Use the following procedures to periodically assess the model's performance:

1. Tracking Metrics: Keep an eye on key performance indicators (KPIs) such as recall, accuracy, precision, and F1 score.

2. Drift Detection: Find variations in the distribution of data that could impact the performance of the model. External circumstances or changing user behavior may be the cause of this.

3. Re-Training: To keep the model accurate and current, retrain it with fresh data on a regular basis.

Addressing Bias

Unfair and discriminating results can result from bias in AI models. To deal with prejudice:

- Data Auditing: Examine training data on a regular

basis to ensure balance and representation. To avoid bias, make sure databases are extensive and diverse.

- Fairness measures: Use fairness measures to evaluate and reduce prejudice. Disparate impact, equalized odds, and demographic parity are a few examples.

- Bias Mitigation Techniques: Reducing bias can be accomplished by using methods including algorithmic tweaks, re-weighting, and re-sampling.

- Openness: Preserve openness in the model's decision-making procedure. Record the model setups, training procedures, and data sources.

6.4 Explainable AI (XAI): Bringing Transparency to AI Decisions

The goal of explainable AI (XAI) is to improve responsibility and trust by making AI judgments comprehensible to humans. For applications where judgments affect specific people or necessitate regulatory compliance, XAI is essential.

Importance of Explainability:

- Trust and Transparency: If users and stakeholders are aware of the decision-making process, they are more inclined to trust AI systems.

- Regulatory Compliance: To comply with regulations, sectors such as banking and healthcare frequently demand justifications for AI-driven choices.

- Ethical AI: Guarantees that AI is used ethically by establishing transparent and responsible decision-making procedures.

Methods for Explainable AI:

1. Feature Importance: Determines which features have the greatest bearing on the predictions made by the model. LIME (Local Interpretable Model-agnostic Explanations) and SHAP (Shapley Additive Explanations) are two methods.

2. Model Visualization: Offers a visual representation of the inner workings of the model. Neural network heatmaps and decision trees are two examples.

3. Utilizes

4. Rule-Based Models: Unlike sophisticated models like deep neural networks, rule-based systems like decision trees and linear models are more interpretable by nature.

5. Counterfactual Explanations: Describes how decisions might differ if certain input facts were altered. This aids users in comprehending the bounds of the decision.

Putting XAI into Practice:

- User-Friendly Interfaces: Create interfaces that make explanations understandable and easy to get. To improve understanding, use straightforward language and visual aids.

- Interactive Explanations: Let people engage with explanations, investigate various situations, and pose inquiries concerning the behavior of the model.

- Ongoing Enhancement: Get input on explanations to make them more understandable and practical. To improve transparency, update and improve the model on a regular basis.

Organizations may create reliable, equitable, and transparent AI systems by carefully choosing the right AI model, closely adhering to the model training procedure, keeping an eye on performance, reducing bias, and putting explainable AI strategies into practice. This all-encompassing strategy guarantees that AI models not only function properly but also win over users' and stakeholders' trust and confidence, which results in more impactful and successful AI applications.

CHAPTER 7

Building and honing your AI model

There's more to integrating AI into current workflows than just turning on a new device. It calls for careful planning, smooth integration, easy-to-use interfaces, efficient change management, and a dedication to ongoing development. You will be guided through these crucial measures to guarantee a successful integration of AI in this chapter.

7.1 Integrating APIs for Optimal Data Flow and Features

AI integration into current workflows requires the use of Application Programming Interfaces (APIs). Through APIs, various software systems can interact with one another, facilitating smooth functionality and data flow.

1. Comprehending APIs: APIs are collections of tools and protocols that enable communication between

various software programs. When it comes to AI, APIs can be utilized for:

2.

3. Link your apps to outside artificial intelligence (AI) services, such as machine learning models, picture recognition, and natural language processing.

4. Include AI Models: Integrate bespoke AI models with your current frameworks.

5. Workflow Automation: Automate repetitive tasks like data collecting, analysis, and decision-making to streamline processes.

Putting API Integration Into Practice:

1. Find Integration Points: Figure out how AI can improve your current processes. Seek out activities that can be improved using AI or automated.

2. Select the Appropriate APIs: Choose APIs based on what you require. Take into account elements like support, documentation, functionality, and ease of use.

3. Construct and Examine: To integrate the selected APIs, collaborate with your development team. To

make sure the integration functions easily and consistently, do extensive testing.

4. Safety and Adherence: Make sure that any data sent through APIs is encrypted. Protect sensitive data by putting authentication, encryption, and other security measures in place.

Instances of API Integration:

1. Customer service: You can handle frequently asked questions and give prompt answers by integrating a chatbot API into your customer service platform.

2. Sales & Marketing: Customizing product recommendations for clients based on their browsing and purchasing history through the use of an AI-powered recommendation API.

3. Healthcare: Putting into practice an API for medical imaging analysis to help radiologists diagnose diseases using MRIs and X-rays.

7.2 Design Considerations for User Interface (UI) and User Experience (UX)

AI needs to be easy to utilize in order for workflows to properly include it. In order to make sure that consumers can engage with AI-powered devices with ease, UI and UX design are essential.

UI and UX Design Fundamentals:

1. Simplicity: Make sure the UI is clear and easy to use. Keep things simple and concentrate on the functionality that users really need.
2. Intuitivity: Create an interface that requires little to no training for people to grasp and operate. Employ well-known design patterns and concise labeling.
3. Retain a uniform design throughout the application to ensure consistency. Maintaining consistency in layout, typefaces, and colors makes consumers feel more at ease and lowers the learning curve.
4. Feedback: Give users' activities prompt, understandable feedback. Error notifications, progress indicators, and confirmation messages are a few examples of this.
5. Accessibility: Make certain that all users, including those with impairments, can easily interact with the

design. To ensure that everyone can use your AI-powered solution, adhere to accessibility rules.

Using AI to Improve User Experience:

1. Personalization: Tailor the user experience with AI. Adjust interfaces, content, and recommendations according to user preferences and behavior.

2. Automation: Automate repeated actions to simplify chores. Use AI, for instance, to automate data entry, propose answers, and fill out forms automatically.

3. AI can be used to give predictive help, such as predicting user needs and providing pertinent recommendations or notifications.

4. Natural Language Interaction: Use conversational language to enable users to communicate with the system through the use of natural language processing.

Creating with Transparency and Trust in Mind:

1. Explainability: Provide justifications for AI judgments to increase transparency. Assist users in

comprehending the reasoning behind the AI's recommendations or decisions.

2. Control: Give users authority over AI functions. Give them the option to change settings, accept or reject certain features, and submit feedback.

3. Security: Consider security when designing. Safeguard user information and make sure privacy is upheld.

7.3 Methods of Change Management for User Acceptance

For users, integrating AI into current workflows can mean a big shift. In order to minimize opposition and promote easy acceptance, effective change management tactics are important.

Principles of Change Management:

1. Communication: Inform users of any changes. Describe the advantages of integrating AI, how it will affect their work, and what to anticipate from the changeover.

2. Instruction and Assistance: Give users thorough instruction so they can operate the new AI-powered tools. Provide continuing assistance to resolve any queries or problems.

3. Involve users in the process of implementation. Consult with them, respond to their worries, and take their suggestions into consideration for future developments.

4. Support for Leadership: Make sure the move has the active backing of the leadership. Leaders have the ability to promote the advantages of integrating AI and foster acceptance across their teams.

How to Manage Change Successfully:

1. Determine Readiness: Determine how prepared the company is to integrate AI. Determine possible obstacles and create plans to overcome them.

2. Create a Strategy: Make a thorough change management strategy that specifies the actions, deadlines, and materials needed for the shift.

3. Pilot Programs: To test AI integration in a controlled setting, begin with pilot programs. After receiving

comments, making any improvements, and showcasing accomplishments, roll out to the entire organization.

4. Observe and Modify: Keep a close eye on the adoption process and be ready to make changes as necessary. Keep lines of communication open and swiftly address any difficulties that may arise.

Getting Past Resistance:

1. Face Fears: Address frequent concerns and misunderstandings regarding AI, such as the possibility of losing control or losing jobs. Stress that AI should complement human abilities rather than take their place.

2. Emphasize Advantages: Pay attention to how AI benefits users' jobs. Demonstrate how AI may help people focus on higher-value jobs by eliminating menial duties and increasing productivity.

3. Offer Rewards: Reward early adopters and those who use the new system actively with incentives. Acknowledge and honor their work.

7.4 Iterative Enhancement and Feedback Loops

AI integration is a continuous process rather than a one-time occurrence. AI systems must be improved continuously in order to continue meeting user needs. Feedback loops and continuous development are essential for this.

Creating Feedback Loops

1. Frequent Surveys and Interviews: Ask users about their experiences using the AI-powered system through frequent surveys and interviews. Make use of these comments to pinpoint places that need work.

2. Analyze user behavior and interactions with the system using user analytics. Examine consumption trends, locate bottlenecks, and find areas that could be improved.

3. Channels of Support: Give users a variety of ways to voice concerns, submit suggestions for improvement, and report problems. Help desks, chat assistance, and feedback forms are a few examples of this.

Process of Continuous Improvement:

1. Iterative Development: Use an iterative development strategy in which performance metrics and user input are used to guide small, gradual improvements. This makes it possible to continuously improve and refine.

2. Performance Monitoring: Keep an eye on how well AI systems and models are working. Monitor important KPIs, spot deviations, and take quick action to resolve problems.

3. Continual Updates: Provide frequent updates for the AI system that include bug patches, performance improvements, and new functionality. Inform users of any updates or modifications.

4. Acknowledging Mistakes: View setbacks as chances for growth. To avoid a recurrence, evaluate what went wrong, pinpoint the underlying cause, and put corrective measures in place.

Establishing an Environment of Constant Improvement:

1. Promote Innovation: Establish an environment that welcomes experimentation and creativity. Permit groups to experiment with novel concepts and methods for utilizing AI.

2. Encourage cooperation amongst various teams, such as those composed of business analysts, data scientists, AI developers, and end users. More efficient solutions may result from cross-functional cooperation.

3. Education and Training: Make a continuous investment in your team's training and growth. Provide them with regular updates on the newest AI tools, technologies, and best practices.

4. Careful planning, user-centric design, efficient change management, and a dedication to continuous improvement are necessary for integrating AI into current operations. Organizations can successfully employ AI to improve operations, increase efficiency, and provide better results for their users and stakeholders by adhering to these criteria.

CHAPTER 8

Assessing Your AI Implementation's Success

Understanding the effects of AI, making wise decisions, and guaranteeing ongoing progress all depend on measuring the implementation's performance. You will learn how to define pertinent Key Performance Indicators (KPIs), monitor AI performance metrics, carry out A/B testing for optimization, and recognize and handle unexpected results in this chapter.

8.1 Specifying Goal-Aligned Key Performance Indicators (KPIs)

KPIs, or key performance indicators, are crucial measurements that assist you in gauging the effectiveness of an AI deployment. It's important to define the appropriate KPIs that are in line with your business objectives so that you can monitor development, assess efficacy, and make informed decisions.

KPI Understanding: KPIs are measurable indicators of an organization's or project's essential success components. KPIs for AI deployment should be closely linked to the precise goals you want to accomplish.

Aligning KPIs with Objectives

Identify Business Objectives: To begin, determine which primary business goals the AI installation is meant to assist. This could be raising income, decreasing expenses, raising operational effectiveness, or enhancing customer pleasure.

Assign precise and quantifiable KPIs: Establish SMART (specific, measurable, achievable, relevant, and time-bound) key performance indicators. This guarantees that your measurement efforts are clear and focused.

Connect AI Use Cases with KPIs: Link every KPI to the particular AI use cases or features you have put in place. For example, if you have implemented an AI-driven chatbot, a pertinent key performance indicator could be the decrease in the mean time taken to respond to client inquiries.

KPIs Related to Artificial Intelligence:

1. Accuracy: The proportion of accurate predictions or classifications produced by the AI model.
2. Precision and Recall: Recall gauges the capacity to recognize every pertinent event, whereas precision gauges the accuracy of positive predictions.
3. Response Time: The amount of time AI systems require to comprehend and react to inputs.
4. Cost Savings: The decrease in operating expenses brought about by automation powered by AI.
5. Customer Satisfaction: Increases in Net Promoter levels (NPS) or customer satisfaction levels after AI technologies are implemented.
6. Employee Productivity: Enhanced output from AI tools that automate monotonous activities.

8.2 Measuring and Tracking AI Performance

In order to make sure that your AI models are producing the expected outcomes and staying in line with business objectives, tracking and monitoring AI performance metrics is essential.

Installing Monitoring Systems

1. Automatic Monitoring: Put in place automatic monitoring systems to keep tabs on AI performance indicators all the time. Real-time analytics systems and dashboards are examples of tools that can offer current insights.

2. Notifications and Alerts: Create alerts to tell you when performance metrics significantly change or deviate. This enables prompt action in the event that problems emerge.

Key Metrics to Track:

1. Model Accuracy: Verify your AI models' accuracy on a regular basis. Make sure they are reliably classifying or predicting the right things.

2. Performance Over Time: Monitor trends in performance over time to spot trends, advancements, or regressions in AI capacity.

3. Data Quality: Keep an eye on the input data's

quality. To keep the model performing as intended, make sure the data is correct, up to date, and tidy.

4. System Efficiency: Calculate the uptime, processing speeds, and resource usage of the system. Make sure AI systems don't create any obstacles to their seamless operation.

Feedback Loops

1. User Feedback: Gather user opinions about AI systems that they deal with. Utilize these comments to pinpoint areas that need work and improve the user experience.

2. Details of Error: Examine mistakes and misclassifications to determine the root reasons. This aids in accuracy improvement and model refinement.

8.3 Continuous Optimization through A/B Testing

By contrasting two iterations of a system to see which works better, A/B testing, also known as split testing, is a potent technique for optimizing AI systems.

What A/B Testing Means: A/B testing is splitting up your user base into two groups.

- One group uses the AI system's current version (A),
- while the other group uses its new version (B).

You can ascertain which version yields superior results by comparing the results.

A/B Testing Procedure Steps

1. Define the Hypothesis: Clearly state your goals and objectives for the test. You may speculate, for instance, that a new algorithm may speed up response times.

2. Choose Metrics: Select the performance measures (accuracy, user satisfaction, processing time, etc.) that will be used to assess the test.

3. Choose Random Groups: Assign users at random to the A and B groups in order to guarantee impartial outcomes.

4. Conduct the Exam: Allow both groups to engage with their respective versions of the AI system for a certain amount of time to carry out the A/B test.

5. Examine Outcomes: To find out which version

performs better, compare the two groups' performance metrics. To guarantee that the outcomes are noteworthy, employ statistical analysis.

6. Apply Modifications: Determine whether to keep the current version (A) or adopt the new version (B) based on the results. Make any required adjustments to enhance performance overall.

A/B Testing Benefits:

1. Data-Driven Decisions: A/B testing lessens reliance on assumptions or intuition by supporting decisions with empirical data.

2. Continuous Improvement: Regular A/B testing allows AI systems to be optimized and improved over time.

3. Risk Mitigation: Lowering the chance of unfavorable effects is achieved by testing changes before they are fully implemented.

8.4 Recognizing and Handling Unexpected Results

Artificial Intelligence deployments can result in

unanticipated consequences even with meticulous planning. Maintaining the efficacy and dependability of your AI systems depends on quickly recognizing and resolving these difficulties.

Common Unexpected Outcomes:

1. Model Drift: As data patterns or outside influences alter over time, AI models' performance may deteriorate. We call this model drift.

2. Bias and Fairness Issues: AI models may unintentionally acquire biases, producing results that are unjust or discriminatory.

3. Performance Degradation: Unexpected interactions, inefficiencies in the system, and problems with data quality can all lead to a decrease in performance.

Actions to Take in Response to Unexpected Outcomes:

1. frequent Audits: Examine AI models on a frequent basis to spot any indications of model drift or declining performance. Examine current performance indicators in relation to past standards.

2. Bias Detection: Use fairness and bias detection techniques to keep an eye out for any indications of bias in AI models. Make that training data impartial and representative by reviewing and updating it on a regular basis.

3. Root Cause Analysis: Examine the fundamental causes of unexpected events by doing a root cause analysis. Examining data sources, model settings, and system interactions are all part of this process.

4. Iterative Refinement: Make incremental improvements to AI models by utilizing the knowledge gathered from audits and root cause studies. When necessary, update algorithms, retrain models, and modify settings.

5. Involve Stakeholders: Involve stakeholders in recognizing and resolving unexpected consequences, such as end users and domain experts. Their observations can offer insightful context and support the creation of workable solutions.

Preventive Actions

1. Scenario Testing: Run scenario tests to mimic

different scenarios and spot possible problems before they arise in practical applications.

2. Continuous Learning: Put in place frameworks for continuous learning so that AI models can pick up new information and adjust to shifting circumstances.

3. Openness and Recordkeeping: Keep AI judgments and procedures transparent. To maintain accountability, track updates, modifications, and the rationale behind them.

Determining pertinent KPIs, monitoring performance metrics, running A/B tests, and dealing with unexpected results are all necessary steps in assessing the effectiveness of AI implementation. By taking these actions, businesses can make sure that their AI systems produce valuable, dependable, and consistent outcomes, fostering ongoing development and optimizing AI's advantages.

CHAPTER 9

Trends and Ethical Issues in the Future of AI

Artificial Intelligence (AI) is a field that is fast developing and has a bright future, but it also presents substantial ethical challenges. The upcoming technologies, the necessity of ethical AI development and application, the crucial concerns of algorithmic bias and fairness, and the possible effects of AI on employment and the nature of labor in the future are all covered in this chapter.

9.1 New Developments in AI Technology

Artificial intelligence (AI) is a dynamic subject where ongoing breakthroughs and discoveries are changing how humans interact with technology. To stay ahead of the curve in the field of artificial intelligence, one must comprehend these new tendencies.

Important New AI Technologies:

1. Generative AI: Developments in generative AI, particularly transformer-based models like GPT and Generative Adversarial Networks (GANs), are making it possible to produce high-caliber synthetic content, such as text, photos, and videos. Applications for these technologies can be found in entertainment, content production, and even medication research.

2. The Use of AI in Edge Computing More and more AI is being used at the edge, near the source of data. Real-time decision-making is made possible, privacy is improved, and latency is decreased. IoT devices with AI capabilities found in smart cities and households are one example.

3. Intelligent AI (XAI): Transparency and interpretability are becoming more and more important as AI systems get more complicated. The goal of explainable AI is to increase accountability and trust by making AI judgments comprehensible to humans.

4. Learning Reinforcement (RL): In reinforcement learning (RL), agents pick up decision-making skills through interactions with their surroundings. Developments in RL are propelling innovations in robotics, self-driving cars, and AI for gaming.

5. AI in Medical: Through its use in predictive analytics, personalized medicine, and diagnostics, artificial intelligence (AI) is completely changing the healthcare industry. AI is capable of drug discovery support, patient outcome prediction, and medical imaging analysis.

Next Trends:

1. Quantum artificial intelligence: AI combined with quantum computing holds the promise of solving complicated issues far more quickly than with traditional computers. Complex system modeling, material science, and cryptography could all be completely transformed by quantum AI.

2. Partnership Between AI and Humans: Instead of trying to replace human abilities, future AI systems will increasingly concentrate on enhancing them. Professionals across a range of industries will benefit from collaborative AI technologies, which will boost output and innovation.

3. Governance and Ethics in AI: The increasing prevalence of AI will lead to a greater focus on ethical standards and governance structures to guarantee responsible AI development and application.

9.2 Conscientious AI Development and Application

The goal of responsible AI development is to build and apply AI systems in a way that is morally just, equitable, and advances society. This entails taking into account AI's wider effects on people and communities.

Responsible AI Principles:

1. Openness: AI systems ought to operate in a

transparent manner. Users ought to be aware of the data being used and the decision-making process. This promotes accountability and trust.

2. Equity: Fairness and the absence of bias should be built into AI design. This entails identifying and reducing any discrimination present in datasets and AI systems.

3. Privacy: Ensuring the privacy of users is crucial. AI systems should adhere to applicable privacy laws and be built with robust data protection safeguards.

4. Responsibility: Organizations and developers need to take responsibility for the AI systems they build. This entails taking accountability for the results and mitigating any unfavorable effects.

5. Inclusivity: All people should be able to use AI, regardless of their financial situation, gender, color, or ability. This objective can be met in part by guaranteeing varied participation in AI development teams.

Actionable AI Development Steps:

1. Ethical Principles: Provide precise ethical standards and guiding concepts for the creation and application of AI. These ought to be in line with both society norms and the organization's larger values.

2.

3. Multicultural Teams: To work on AI initiatives, put together varied teams. Diverse viewpoints can aid in spotting potential biases and guaranteeing the inclusivity and fairness of AI systems.

4.

5. Impact Evaluation: Evaluate the possible effects of AI systems by conducting in-depth impact evaluations. This entails taking the effects on the environment, economy, and society into account.

6.

7. Stakeholder Engagement: Consult with relevant parties, such as users, experts, and impacted groups, to get their input and make sure AI systems live up to their expectations.

8.

9. Ongoing Surveillance: Establish methods for ongoing assessment and monitoring to keep tabs on the effectiveness and influence of AI systems. This enables prompt modifications and enhancements.

9.3 Fairness and Algorithmic Bias in AI Systems

When AI systems generate biased results, frequently reflecting or exaggerating pre existing societal biases, this is known as algorithmic bias. Achieving equal results and fostering trust in AI depend on ensuring fairness.

Knowing What Algorithmic Bias Is

1. Data Bias: Artificial intelligence models are educated on potentially biased data. The AI system may reinforce biases if the training data contains historical disparities.

2. An Inherent Bias: Biases may be introduced during the algorithm's design and execution. This may occur if the model has biased presumptions or if some groups are underrepresented.

3. Interaction Prejudice: Another source of bias is user interaction with AI systems. For instance, prejudices based on user behavior and preferences may be reinforced by search engines.

Tackling Algorithmic Disparities:

1. Multiple Data Gathering: Make that all pertinent groups are represented in the training data, which should be diverse. This makes AI models more equitable and balanced.

2. Tools for Detecting Biases: Employ methods and instruments to identify and quantify bias in AI systems. Audit AI models frequently to find and fix biases.

3. Restrictions on Fairness: As you design the model, take fairness limitations into consideration. This may entail establishing precise fairness objectives and optimizing models to satisfy them.

1. Human Oversight: Put in place procedures for human oversight in order to examine and confirm AI choices. Human judgment can guarantee fair decisions and assist in identifying biases.

2. Accountability and Transparency: Keep the data and methods utilized in AI systems open and transparent. Take ownership of the results and assume responsibility for rectifying any skewed consequences.

9.4 AI's Effect on Employment and the Future of Work

AI is changing the nature of employment and the labor market. Artificial intelligence (AI) raises concerns about job displacement and the need for new skills, even while it also has the potential to increase productivity and open up new opportunities.

AI's Beneficial Effects on Employment:

1. Automation of Tasks That Recur: AI can automate monotonous and routine jobs, freeing up workers to

concentrate on higher-value work. Increased productivity and job satisfaction may result from this.

2. Creation of the Job: AI is generating new industries and job roles. For instance, there is a rising need for data scientists, AI ethicists, and AI specialists.

3. Improved Judgment-Taking: AI solutions can help decision-making processes and offer insights, empowering staff members to make better-informed choices.

4. Enhanced Productivity: AI can streamline workflows and procedures, increasing productivity and reducing costs. This may spur company expansion and generate more job openings.

Difficulties and Points to Remember:

1. Relocation of Job: Some industries may experience job displacement as a result of task automation. It's critical to oversee this change and provide impacted

employees with programs for upskilling and retraining.

2. Deficit in Skills: The need for AI-related abilities is rising, and there can be a skills gap in the labor force. In order to equip workers for the AI-driven economy, it is imperative to invest in education and training programs.

3. Inequality: Adoption of AI could make inequality already present worse if gains are not shared equally. It is crucial to guarantee equitable access to AI possibilities and technologies.

4. Industrial Revolution: AI is transforming the nature of employment, allowing for more flexible and remote work schedules. Companies must help their staff in this new climate and adjust to these changes.

Getting Ready for the Work of the Future:

1. Lifetime Education: Encourage a culture that values ongoing skill development and lifelong learning.

Encourage staff members to adopt new technology and pick up necessary skills.

2. Supportive Policies: Put in place programs and policies that will assist employees in adjusting to new positions and sectors. This involves making instruction, career guidance, and training accessible.

3. Inclusive Growth: Make sure that a large portion of the public benefits from AI. This entails encouraging inclusivity and diversity in the AI workforce and ensuring that AI tools are available to everyone.

4. Ethical Considerations: Talk about how AI affects ethics in the workplace. This entails maintaining ethical labor standards, defending the rights of employees, and promoting a pleasant workplace culture.

AI has enormous promise for the future, but there are also important ethical issues to be aware of. Organizations may embrace the power of AI while guaranteeing favorable and fair outcomes for all stakeholders by being up to date on developing technologies, making a commitment to responsible AI development, tackling algorithmic bias, and becoming ready for the future of work.

CHAPTER 10

Final Thoughts: The Potential of AI for Practical Applications

In this last chapter, we consider the potential applications of artificial intelligence (AI) in several industries and its transformative capacity. We go over the essential components of putting effective AI solutions into practice, investigate the revolutionary possibilities of AI, talk about creating a long-term AI plan, and emphasize AI's positive influence on the course of human history.

10.1 A Summary: Applying AI Solutions to Achieve Success

Putting AI ideas into practice requires a methodical strategy to efficiently utilizing technology. The key to success is comprehending business requirements, choosing suitable AI tools, assembling competent teams, and smoothly incorporating AI into current workflows.

Critical Components of AI Solution Implementation

1. Understanding Business Needs: Begin by having a thorough grasp of the goals and difficulties that the business faces that AI can help with. To maximum impact, coordinate AI activities with strategic objectives.

2. Selecting Appropriate AI Tools: Analyze and choose the AI platforms and solutions that best meet your needs. Take into account elements like adaptability, scalability, and compatibility with current systems.

3. Creating a Knowledgeable Team: Invest in assembling a knowledgeable and varied team of engineers, business analysts, and data scientists for your AI project. Encourage a culture of cooperation that rewards creativity and never stops learning.

4. Information as Energy: Acknowledge that data is essential to the operation of AI systems. To guarantee quality and dependability, put strong data

gathering, cleaning, and security procedures in place.

5. Adoption and Integration: AI may be smoothly incorporated into current processes by using user-centric design and efficient API integration. Proactively manage change to increase ROI and encourage user adoption.

6. Monitoring and Improvement: Keep an eye on AI performance metrics at all times, experiment with different combinations to optimize results, and quickly handle unexpected results. To develop AI solutions over time, cultivate a culture of continuous improvement.

10.2 AI's Potential to Transform Various Industries

AI has the power to completely transform a number of businesses by fostering creativity, increasing productivity, and opening up new avenues.

AI's Effect on Various Industries:

1. Medicine: AI is revolutionizing healthcare by enabling diagnosis through medical image analysis, predictive analytics for disease prevention, and personalized treatment.

2. Money: Artificial intelligence (AI) is being used in the financial industry to improve fraud detection, optimize trading algorithms, and improve customer care with chatbots and virtual assistants.

3. Retail: With its predictive analytics for demand forecasting, inventory management optimization, and tailored suggestions, artificial intelligence is transforming the retail industry.

4. Production: Production process optimization, quality control, and downtime reduction are all being enhanced by AI-driven automation.

5. Distribution: AI is improving route planning, enabling autonomous cars, and boosting safety through real-time data processing in the transportation sector.

6. Next Possibilities: The way AI is integrated with new technologies like 5G, blockchain, and IoT will increase how much of an industry-wide transformation it can have.

10.3 Developing a Long-Term Sustainable AI Strategy

In order to effectively utilize artificial intelligence in a sustainable manner, companies need to create a long-term plan that puts morality first, encourages creativity, and makes sure that AI is used responsibly.

A Sustainable AI Strategy's Components:

1. Ethical Principles: Provide precise ethical standards for the creation and application of AI. Encourage openness, justice, responsibility, and diversity in AI projects.

2. Governance Frameworks: Put in place strong governance frameworks to supervise AI initiatives, control risks, and guarantee legal compliance.

3. Ongoing Education: Encourage a culture of ongoing education and skill-building to stay up with AI developments. Spend money on training courses for staff members in every position.

4. Collaboration and Partnerships: To maximize group knowledge and spur AI innovation, collaborate with outside partners, academic institutions, and industry professionals.

5. Risk Management: Recognize and address possible hazards related to AI, such as implications for society, cybersecurity issues, and data privacy.

6. Extended Goals: Create a clear plan for how AI will function inside the company going forward. Evaluate and modify the AI strategy on a regular basis to keep up with changing business requirements and technology developments.

10.4 Embracing the Future: The Positive Potential of AI

In the future, AI has the ability to positively impact society and solve global issues, making it a force for good.

AI as a Positive Force:

1. Personalized treatment plans, drug development, and AI-powered diagnostics can all lead to better healthcare results and more accessibility.

2. Sustainability of the Environment: Through data-driven insights and optimization, artificial intelligence (AI) can promote sustainable practices in resource conservation, energy management, and agriculture.

3. Education and Accessibility: AI-powered personalized learning systems can improve student performance and give everyone in the world fair access to high-quality education.

4.

5. Equity in Society: Inequalities in society can be lessened and decision-making equity can be increased by addressing prejudice in AI systems and fostering inclusivity.

6. Accountability and Guidance: To make sure that AI development prioritizes ethical considerations and serves the greater good, organizations and stakeholders must work together.

7. To sum up, artificial intelligence (AI) has enormous potential to spur innovation, improve productivity, and have a positive social influence on a variety of industries. Through strategic implementation of AI solutions, development of sustainable strategies, and acceptance of AI as a force for good, companies may set the stage for a future in which technology serves the interests of all parties involved and makes the world more inclusive and sustainable.

ABOUT THE AUTHOR

One well-known author and thought leader in the IT space is Taylor Royce. Over the course of a two-decade career, Royce has established himself as a reliable source for tech trend analysis and forecasting, bringing complicated technological ideas within reach of a wide audience. Royce is well-known for his perceptive and innovative work, which spans a broad range of subjects such as blockchain, artificial intelligence, cybersecurity, and the Internet of Things (IoT).

Royce's interest in technology started while he studied computer science, where his early curiosity with the possibilities of computing systems established the groundwork for a long-lasting and intense involvement with the tech industry. Royce's practical expertise in a range of tech professions, from software development to strategic consulting, combined with his academic background to provide him a thorough understanding of the inner workings of the sector.

Taylor Royce has penned multiple best-selling books and contributed to many esteemed tech journals throughout the course of a busy writing career. These pieces are distinguished by their precision, extensive investigation, and capacity to reduce complicated concepts into understandable insights for both IT fans and corporations. Royce's writings have been translated into other languages, demonstrating their popularity and influence around the world.

Aside from writing, Royce frequently appears as a guest on tech-related podcasts and webinars and is in high demand as a speaker at international tech conferences. Because of his increased visibility, Royce has solidified his reputation as a leading expert in the IT sector, frequently consulted for his knowledgeable opinions on cutting-edge technology and their social ramifications.

Royce's work largely addresses the moral and societal ramifications of technological progress. Royce, who promotes ethical tech creation and use, stresses the significance of tackling problems like data privacy, the digital gap, and the moral application of artificial intelligence. Royce's contributions are certain to be both educational and in line with the larger objective of using technology for the greater benefit because of this balanced viewpoint.

Beyond just writing and speaking, Taylor Royce has a significant impact on a number of IT education initiatives and actively mentors upcoming tech workers. This emphasis on developing the next wave of tech innovators demonstrates a commitment to the equitable and sustainable development of the tech sector.

All things considered, Taylor Royce is a well-known personality in the field of technology writing, renowned for his ability to combine technical know-how with careful analysis and a vision of a time when technology will meaningfully and morally serve humankind.

www.ingramcontent.com/pod-product-compliance
Lightning Source LLC
LaVergne TN
LVHW051703050326
832903LV00032B/3986